PIT STOP PREFIXES

By Michael Ruscoe

Cover illustrated by Scott Angle

Interior illustrated by Robert Roper

Language arts curriculum consultant: Debra Voege, M.A.

Gareth Stevens
Publishing

Please visit our web site at **www.garethstevens.com**.
For a free color catalog describing Gareth Stevens Publishing's list of
high-quality books, call 1-800-542-2595 (USA) or 1-800-387-3178 (Canada).
Gareth Stevens Publishing's fax: 1-877-542-2596

Library of Congress Cataloging-in-Publication Data

Ruscoe, Michael.
    Pit stop prefixes / by Michael Ruscoe ; illustrated by Robert Roper ;
language arts curriculum consultant : Debra Voege, M.A.
        p. cm. — (Grammar all-stars: kinds of words)
    At head of title : Grammar all-stars : kinds of words
    ISBN-10: 1-4339-0011-4   ISBN-13: 978-1-4339-0011-2 (lib. bdg.)
    ISBN-10: 1-4339-0152-8   ISBN-13: 978-1-4339-0152-2 (pbk.)
        1. English language—Suffixes and prefixes—Juvenile literature.
2. English language—Word formation—Juvenile literature.   3. English
language—Grammar—Juvenile literature.   I. Voege, Debra.   II. Title.
III. Title: Grammar all-stars : kinds of words.   IV. Series.
PE1175.R87   2008
425'.92—dc22   2008028292

This edition first published in 2009 by
Gareth Stevens Publishing
A Weekly Reader® Company
1 Reader's Digest Road
Pleasantville, NY 10570-7000 USA

Copyright © 2009 by Gareth Stevens, Inc.

Executive Managing Editor: Lisa M. Herrington
Senior Editor: Barbara Bakowski
Creative Director: Lisa Donovan
Art Director: Ken Crossland
Publisher: Keith Garton

Printed in the United States of America

1 2 3 4 5 6 7 8 9 10 09 08

CONTENTS

Look for the **boldface** words on each page.
Then read the **TRACK TIP** that follows.

CHAPTER 1

START YOUR ENGINES!

What Are Prefixes?

"Testing!" P-L-A-Y TV announcer Buzz Starr speaks into his microphone. "Jeff, can you hear me?"

"I can, loud and clear," says Jeff from Pit Row.

"Great!" says Buzz. A moment later, the cameras start rolling. "Hi, folks! Buzz Star here, at the Speedway 200. Kid reporter Jeff Jordan will help me cover today's race. Welcome, Jeff!"

"Hi, Buzz!" says Jeff. "I am **impatient** for the race to start. I hope to see some **nonstop** action!"

"Jeff knows a lot about racing," Buzz says. "He is the national **preteen** Soapbox Derby champion. He is in the area where pit crews service the race cars. What do you think of Pit Row, Jeff?"

"I race soapbox cars," Jeff says. "I was **unaware** of the work that goes into racing real cars!"

"Oh, yes," says Buzz. "What happens *before* a race can change the outcome of the event!"

"Hmm," says Jeff. "That sounds a lot like prefixes."

"Prefixes?" asks Buzz. "How so?"

"A prefix is a letter or group of letters placed before a base word," says Jeff. "When you put a prefix in front of a word, it changes the meaning."

"Wow!" says Buzz. "A kid who knows racing *and* grammar! How **refreshing**!" He looks at his watch. "We don't have much time left before the first lap. Let's quickly **preview** today's action."

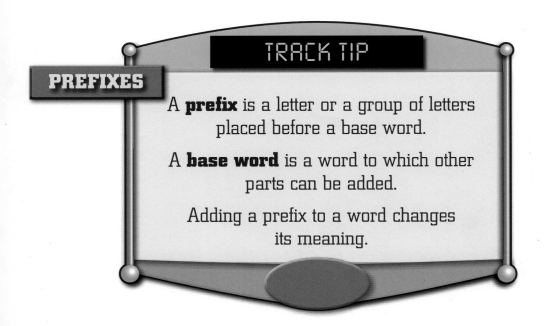

PREFIXES

TRACK TIP

A **prefix** is a letter or a group of letters placed before a base word.

A **base word** is a word to which other parts can be added.

Adding a prefix to a word changes its meaning.

"Right," says Jeff. "There are so many great drivers in the race. It's **impossible** to guess who will win."

"Doug Dragster has the pole position," Buzz says. "That is the best place to start the race. Doug won't be **unhappy** with his spot!"

DOUG DRAGSTER #3

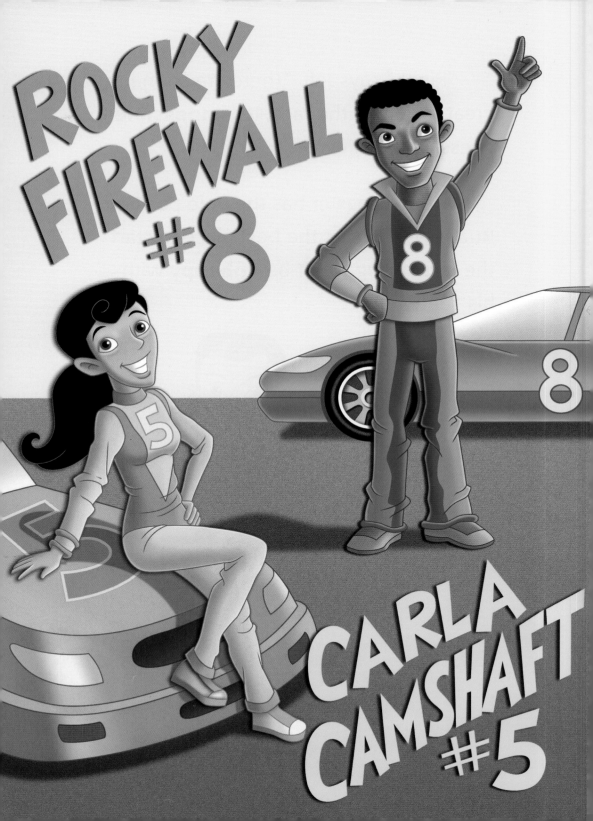

"Rocky Firewall is racing today," says Jeff. "He's an **unlikely** winner."

"I **disagree**," Buzz says. "That's **illogical**. Rocky was **unbeaten** last year."

"That's true," Jeff admits. "But his driving has been **inconsistent** lately."

"Carla Camshaft is also in the race today," Buzz adds. "She was one of the first female champs. That puts the other drivers at a **disadvantage**."

PREFIXES THAT CAN MEAN "NOT"

TRACK TIP

Some common prefixes are **dis-, il-, im-, in-, ir-, non-,** and **un-**. These prefixes usually mean "**not**."

BILLY ROLLBAR #6

"Wedge Wheeler is in the race, too," says Jeff. "He really **misbehaves** on the track. This race might be a **mismatch**!"

"The hometown favorite is Billy Rollbar," says Buzz. "Let's listen to his **pretaped** interview with our own Jeff Jordan."

"Billy, what can you say to **reassure** your fans?" asks Jeff.

"My crew has **rebuilt** my car's engine," Billy says. "It runs perfectly."

"Billy, are you having any **prerace** jitters?"

"Well, Jeff, don't **misquote** me. I'm not promising a win," says Billy. "But I feel like a champ today!"

"Back to you, Buzz!" Jeff says.

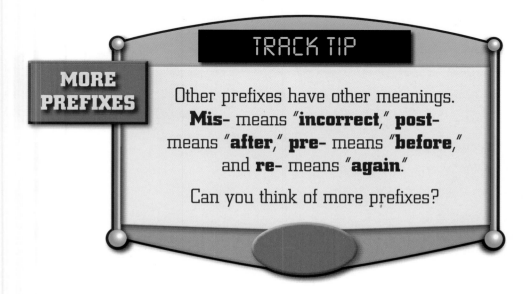

TRACK TIP

MORE PREFIXES

Other prefixes have other meanings. **Mis-** means "**incorrect**," **post-** means "**after**," **pre-** means "**before**," and **re-** means "**again**."

Can you think of more prefixes?

Buzz points to the snack bar sign **overhead**. "Before the race begins, I'm going to get a hot dog ... or two," he says. "But I have to be careful not to **overeat**. I don't look **underfed**! And I'm certainly not **underweight**!" He smiles and pats his stomach. "Stay with us, folks. We'll be back as the drivers start their engines!"

TRACK TIP

MULTIPLE MEANINGS

Some prefixes have more than one meaning. **Over-** means "**too much**" or "**above.**" **Under-** means "**not enough**" or "**below.**"

CHAPTER 2

BEHIND THE WHEEL

Using Prefixes

Jeff joins Buzz in the broadcast booth.

"We're back with P-L-A-Y TV's coverage of the Speedway 200. There's the green flag," Buzz says. "The race has started!"

"Carla Camshaft jumps out to an early lead," Jeff says. "So far, no one has been able to pass her!"

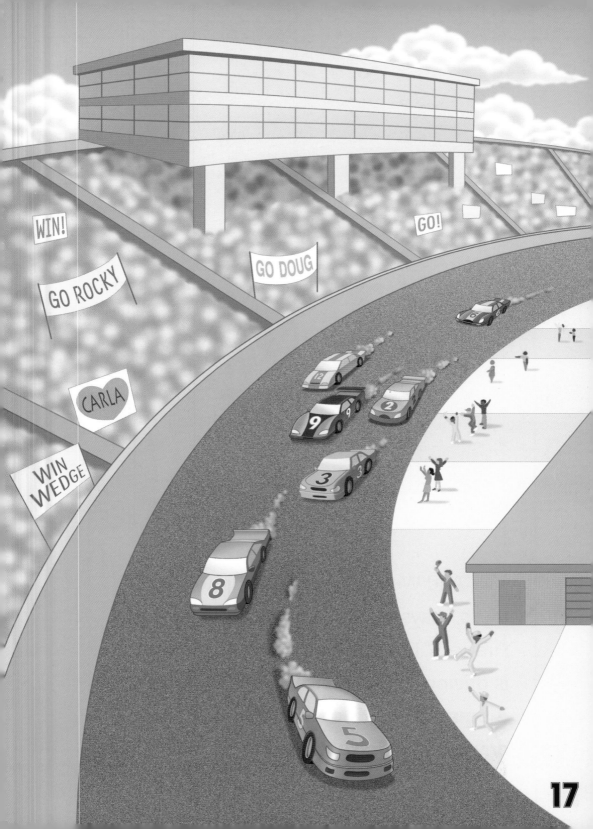

17

"And Wedge Wheeler is up to his old tricks," says Buzz. "He's too close to Rocky Firewall." Buzz shakes his head. "Wedge is driving **irresponsibly**. He should be **disqualified**. It's no wonder the other drivers are **mistrustful** of him."

"Oh! Carla **misjudged** that last turn," says Jeff. "Doug Dragster has passed her."

"At this point, the drivers are **rethinking** their moves," Buzz says. "They can't use up fuel too quickly. If they do, they'll have to make a pit stop. They will lose time **refilling** their tanks."

"Look, Carla is **regaining** the lead," Jeff says excitedly. "She **reappeared** from nowhere."

"Oh, no!" Buzz shouts. "Rocky Firewall has crashed into the wall! The crew is rolling his car off the track!" Buzz frowns. "Folks, Rocky has **discontinued** the race."

"This is an **unexpected** finish for him. What could have happened?" Jeff wonders.

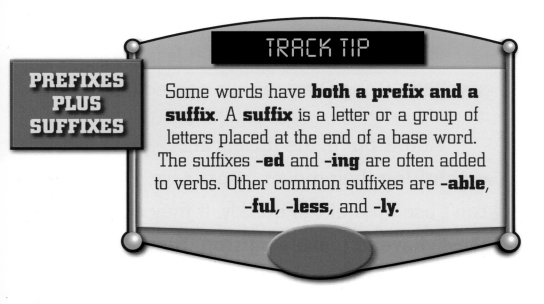

PREFIXES PLUS SUFFIXES

TRACK TIP

Some words have **both a prefix and a suffix**. A **suffix** is a letter or a group of letters placed at the end of a base word. The suffixes **-ed** and **-ing** are often added to verbs. Other common suffixes are **-able**, **-ful**, **-less**, and **-ly**.

"Let's watch it again," says Buzz. "It looks as if Wedge Wheeler bumped Rocky from behind! A crash like that can **disable** a car. No wonder Rocky was **unable** to drive it!"

"His rear axle was **displaced**," Jeff points out. "I hope his crew can have it **replaced** before the next race."

"Meanwhile, Carla pulls in for a pit stop," says Buzz. "Wedge Wheeler will **retake** the lead. No one can **overtake** him now."

"Wedge is going to win the race!" Jeff shouts.

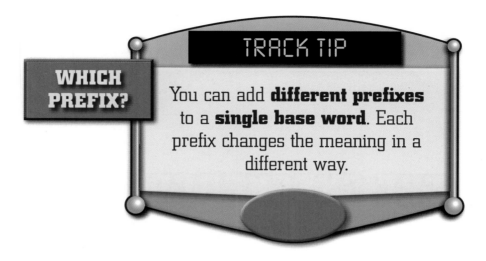

TRACK TIP

You can add **different prefixes** to a **single base word**. Each prefix changes the meaning in a different way.

CHAPTER 3

THE CHECKERED FLAG

Wrap-Up

"Wait!" says Buzz. "Who's coming up on the outside? It's Billy Rollbar! He is closing the **dis**tance! Billy could pass Wedge Wheeler in the final lap."

"Now Wedge is trying to bump Billy," Jeff says. "That's **re**ckless. They could be **in**jured."

"Carla Camshaft is **displeased** with Wedge's tricks," Buzz says. "She is about to **rejoin** the race. She pulls out of the pit— and into Wedge's path!"

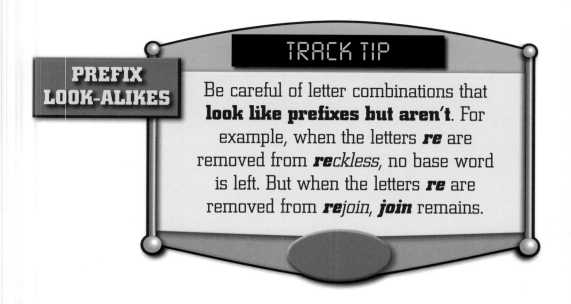

PREFIX LOOK-ALIKES

Be careful of letter combinations that **look like prefixes but aren't**. For example, when the letters **re** are removed from **re**ckless, no base word is left. But when the letters **re** are removed from **re**join, **join** remains.

"That's **insane**!" Jeff covers his eyes. "I can't look!"

25

Wedge slams on his brakes and skids. Billy Rollbar flies under the checkered flag. The crowd **unleashes** a mighty roar.

"Billy is the winner!" Buzz shouts. "Let's **replay** that finish."

Jeff **reunites** with Billy in Victory Lane. "Billy, **relive** that last lap for us," Jeff says. "What was it like?"

"It was **incredible**," Billy replies. "Carla is such an **unselfish** racer. I don't know how I'll ever **repay** her!"

"Thanks for the **postrace** comments," says Jeff. "Back to you, Buzz!"

"Well, folks, that's the race," says Buzz. "So, Jeff, how will you **recall** your day at the Speedway 200?"

Jeff smiles and shakes his head in **disbelief**. "It was **unforgettable**!"

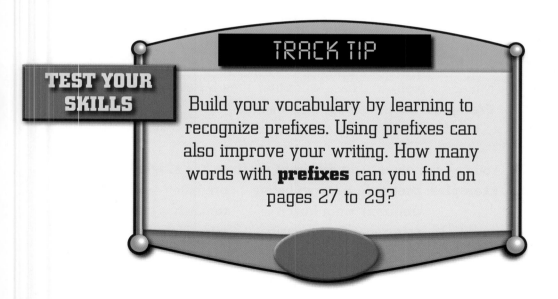

TEST YOUR SKILLS

TRACK TIP

Build your vocabulary by learning to recognize prefixes. Using prefixes can also improve your writing. How many words with **prefixes** can you find on pages 27 to 29?

BUZZ STAR PLAYS BY THE RULES!

A **base word** is a word to which other word parts can be added.
Examples: continue, perfect, direct, sense, judge, school, write, happy

A **prefix** is a letter or group of letters placed before a base word.
Examples: dis- ("not")   im- ("not")   in- ("not")
mis- ("incorrectly")   non- ("not")   pre- ("before")
re- ("again")   un- ("not")

Adding a prefix **changes** a base word's **meaning**.
Examples: **dis**continue = not continue   **im**perfect = not perfect
indirect = not direct   **non**sense = not sense
misjudge = judge incorrectly   **pre**school = before school
rewrite = write again   **un**happy = not happy

A **suffix** is a letter or group of letters placed after a base word. You can add a prefix to a base word that already has a suffix.
Examples: **un**suspect**ing**, **im**perfect**ly**

You can sometimes add **different prefixes** to a **single base word**.
Examples: **pre**frozen = frozen before   **pre**match = match before
unfrozen = not frozen   **re**match = match again
refrozen = frozen again   **mis**match = wrongly match

Don't be fooled by letter combinations that **look like prefixes but are not prefixes**.
Examples: *re*veal, *dis*cuss, *mis*erable

Kid reporter Jeff Jordan posted a story about the race on his blog.
On a piece of paper, **list the words with prefixes**.

SEARCH BLOG | ◀FLAG BLOG | NEXT BLOG

My Day at the Speedway 200

Hi, everybody! I'm Jeff Jordan. I had an unbelievable day at the Speedway 200. The race was nonstop action.

Most of the crowd was rooting for the hometown favorite, Billy Rollbar. Billy won the race, despite some improper moves by Wedge Wheeler. Billy owes thanks to Carla Camshaft. She reappeared in the race at the last minute! Wedge was unable to retake the lead. It was an unlikely finish! Billy pulled off a nearly impossible win.

It would be incorrect to think the drivers will let the contest end there. Don't misjudge them! Both Wedge and Carla dislike losing. Each driver will try to reclaim the top spot in the next event. I can't wait for that rematch!

For a replay of Speedway 200 highlights, visit the P-L-A-Y TV web site. You can also revisit this blog for a preview of the next big race. Remember: Always buckle up!

Posted by Jeff Jordan at 7:10 P.M.

All-Star Challenge

List all the words with a prefix that means "**not**."

Turn the page to check your answers and to see how many points you scored!

ANSWER KEY

Where did you finish in the race?

0–4 prefixes: You Stalled! **9–12** prefixes: Fine Finish!

5–8 prefixes: Flat Tire! **13–16** prefixes: CHECKERED FLAG!

WORDS WITH PREFIXES

1. unbelievable
2. nonstop
3. improper
4. reappeared
5. unable
6. retake

7. unlikely
8. impossible
9. incorrect
10. misjudge
11. dislike
12. reclaim

13. rematch
14. replay
15. revisit
16. preview

All-Star Challenge

1. unbelievable
2. nonstop
3. improper
4. unable

5. unlikely
6. impossible
7. incorrect
8. dislike